How to Take the Risk Out of Sales: Everything Does Not Depend On a Single Sale

Category: Business & Economics

Author: Bob Oros

Publisher: Bob Oros Publishing

ISBN: 978-1-387-20121-1

Copyright 2017

Description: The risk that an insurance company takes on one policyholder is highly unpredictable. Yet the insurance business itself is the safest investment you can make. The risk an insurance company takes on one individual policyholder is tremendous, yet the risk involved in 100,000 policyholders is so predictable it can be figured to the fourth decimal point. Learn how to apply this strategy to your sales.

Key words: sales coaching, sales techniques, job in sales, sales manager training, manufacturing sales training, wholesale sales training, distributor sales training, food service sales,

ISBN 978-1-387-20121-1

90000

9 781387 201211

1. How can you take the risk out of selling?

The trouble with a great many people is that they are not willing to make present sacrifices for future gain.

They prefer to have a good time as they go along, rather than spend time in self-improvement. They have a vague wish to improve their selling skills, but few have that intense desire which motivates them to make sacrifices today for their future.

They have a desire for success, but their desire is not the kind that makes them willing to pay a price or make any sacrifice for accomplishing it. So the majority slide along in mediocrity their entire career. They have ability for something higher, but they don't have the energy and determination to prepare for it. They don't choose to make the necessary effort.

They prefer to take life easier rather than to work for something better. They don't play the game for all they are worth. It is not a lack of ability that holds these sales people down, but a lack of ambition.

By not understanding the science of selling they let fear of rejection hold them back and keep them from becoming their best. They live or die with each sales presentation.

Read this next paragraph carefully...

The next time you become jittery because selling is such a risky business, consider this: The risk that an insurance company takes on one individual policyholder is the most unpredictable thing in the world. What could be more risky than trying to guess when one certain individual is going to have an accident or become sick, or how long he or she is going to live? Yet the insurance business itself is the most stable in the country, the safest investment anyone can make, the nearest thing to a "sure thing" in the way of guaranteed returns to investors. The risk an insurance company takes on one individual policyholder is tremendous, yet the risk involved in 100,000 policyholders is so predictable it can be figured to the fourth decimal point.

Whether or not you will sell any SINGLE prospect is unpredictable. But do as the insurance companies do; "spread the risk" by making a sufficient number of presentations. Make enough calls, see enough prospects, and a number of sales are guaranteed.

Let's say you are calling on 40 customers every week. Instead of going in and just asking for their regular order, make a presentation to each customer on at least four specific items they are not buying from you. That will total 8,000 presentations per year. Let's say you sell half of them and the average order per line item is $100 per week. That will total $400,000 in new annual business.

Selling can be done with mathematical certainty when you understand how it works.

The first step is to identify your target customer and determine how many customers it will take to maintain your business. Here is what I mean, using examples from different industries.

Let's say you wanted to sell residential real estate for a living. You would need to stake out an area that has a minimum of 500 houses. If you began a systematic schedule of contacting these 500 homeowners on a monthly basis, some in person, some on the phone, some by mail, and asking for their business, there would be enough houses bought and sold each year to make a living.

Another good example is insurance. You would have to have a list of one thousand households and contact them on a regular basis. There would be enough insurance needs to earn a living.

Both examples depend, of course, on your ability to out sell the competition.

Even a nursing home with 100 beds has to have them filled with residents. If they have 10 empty beds for any length of time their expenses go up and their profits go down. A hospital is in a similar situation. The success of their "selling" is measured by their "occupancy rate." The next time you visit a hospital ask what their occupancy rate is and you will be surprised at how quickly they can give you the percentage. A manufacturer looking for national distribution needs 200 distributors selling their product line.

Looking at a restaurant's business from a mathematical selling perspective can also be measured with precision. A restaurant needing to sell 1,000 meals each week to take in enough money to pay all their expenses needs a customer base of 5,000. A "rule of thumb" for a restaurant is to take one week's business and multiply it times five. Restaurant customers normally rotate their eating out, so we would want to be sure that we had five thousand people "rotating" into our business at least once every five weeks.

The bottom line… By making a certain number of presentations you can adopt the attitude that "I have got nothing to lose" before making a call, instead of telling yourself, "Everything depends on this," you can now tell yourself that "EVERYTHING DOES NOT DEPEND ON THIS."

 You can strike out occasionally and still hit more home runs than anyone else on the team. Say to yourself, "If I do not call on this customer and ask for the order, the sale is lost anyway. If I call on him or her and flop, I will not be any worse off than I am right now, so I have nothing to lose." When you strike out a few times you get over the "fear of failure."

Comments:

I believe when calling on prospects you are building your future. If you see about 25 new prospects in a week and you get 1 of the prospects a week that is 52 new customers a year. It takes a long time to close a new customer; it could take you up to six months. You have to keep working on the customer until they tell you yes or no. Never walk away from a customer until they till you YES or NO. You have to remember if a customer tells you NO it is not personal it is business. Never leave it on the table for the competition to come and take over the presentation. If you want the sale work hard and get it.
Jim Harris

The only thing you risk when you call on a prospect is the cost of travel and the possibility of rejection. You aren't going to be shot or exported to a foreign country. Nobody is going to sell you into slavery or kidnap you. It is simply another answer to the age old question, supply and demand. If you don't ask you certainly won't get the order.

Dave Ferren

This brings up one of the strongest temptations a salesperson has to face everyday – categorizing prospects. I won't call on them because……. Fill in the blank with your favorite excuse. "I have called on them fifty times with no business", "that manager does not like me", "that business is a little out of our area of expertise" and on and on. I sometimes have to force myself to make the call that I think will be a waste of time and occasionally it will turn out productive. This all comes back to disciplining yourself, keeping your competitive spirit and staying ambitious…easy to say but a constant challenge.

Crocker Smith

You can take the risk out of selling by getting better and better at your job. We all know to expect rejection, and move on. That will make the successes that much sweeter. This story reminds me of when I was in labor having contractions. I was told that after one contraction passes, just say to yourself you are one step closer to final outcome. Same for a rejection, after you are rejected each time, say good, one more down I'm one step closer to the success.

Kimberly Burgess

Selling is like anything else, it's a numbers game. The more calls you make, the more appointments you get, the more presentations you give, the more sales you close. I know a lot of GREAT salespeople, but I don't know of any that have a 100% first approach closing ratio, so what this means for them all is increased front end numbers to support the back end numbers.

Scott Green

This is something that I have implemented recently. I used to put a lot of pressure on myself with each new potential client. Sometimes it might take 20 sales calls to 20 different prospects before I make a sale. It really depends on how much I am willing to sacrifice to make a sale. Do you go to one company, get rejected and go back to the office? I think you have to have that failure expectancy and have the ability to shrug it off and move on. I guess if a pond only had 1 fish in it, we would not fish there very often and would not catch that fish for quite some time, if ever.

Jeffrey Mole

I average anywhere from 25-40 in person sales visits a week. Some are to current customers, some are to prospective customers, some are to anyone who will listen. I usually get only ONE interested individual out of 20 in-person visits. This one individual still has to be groomed and molded – meaning credit reference checks, contracts signed, price negotiation, worker's comp computed, etc. EVEN when I complete all these things – sometimes it does not work out. I just keep going, knowing that the next one might be the one who buys.

Angela Brewer

2. Does the customer expect you to close?

The professional KNOWS that it never pays to leave business on the table. You know that to permit the buyer to defer the close, is to leave the sale open for a competitor to come in and harvest the crop that you worked so hard to grow.

The sales person who has polished the technique of closing to professional brilliance knows the fundamental difference between so-called "high pressure" selling and "low pressure". You know the value of intelligent, dramatic, forceful, suggestive closing when you feel in your heart you are rendering a great service by helping the buyer to decide something for the buyer's own good.

You are in a stronger position because you have the advantage of working with an organized plan and objective. After all, every sale is a contest, starting with two strikes on the buyer, because you have the advantage of working with an organized plan and an objective toward which you are steering him or her. The buyer is in the weak position of a follower on the defensive.

The professional has learned by sad experience that failure to close, to permit the decision to be deferred lets the prospect get cold, when they might have been sold by the application of a quiet, smooth-running, graceful closing technique ...

The buyer expects you to close. How do you go about it to polish the close you are now using? The first step is to get a better understanding of what takes place in the mind of the buyer during the closing moments. Since calling on this account you have been developing an IDEA. You have been supporting this IDEA with your sales points, the effect of your personality, the appeal of your products or service, the price, the terms.

This is the time to GIVE HIM OR HER A DELICATE, SUGGESTIVE PUSH toward the order. You have taken him to "a future place" on the magic carpet of imaginary possession, you've held him there with convincing proof. You have answered the last objection. It is time to do what the buyer expects you to do.

After you ask for the order, sliently say to yourself "today's the day!" And your expectations about making the sale and closing the customer will increase.

Here's the story behind the three prowerful words.

On October 6, 1622, a heavily loaded ship belonging to King Philip IV's fleet struck a reef in a sever storm near the Florida Keys. Nearly 300 people lost their lives, and tons of gold, silver, and other precious cargo went to the bottom of the ocean floor.

Finding sunken treasure had been the life long dream of Mel Fisher. And this treasure from the sunken Spanish ship, Nuestra Senora de Atocha, was the one he wanted to find. To secure financing for his venture Mel had to look into the eyes of doubtful investors and persuade them to believe as he believed - that he and his crew could find the sunken treasure.

Every day for SEVENTEEN YEARS Mel would be on the phone to his investors as well as convincing his crew to keep believing in him and the remote possibility that they would find the sunken treasure. Every day he would say the same thing to his investors and to his crew: "Today's the day." "Today's the day."

For seventeen years he did this while his crew criss-crossed the search area, studying the charts, consulting 16th century information and logs, trying one thing and then another, changing strategies as needed and gathering what little knowledge they could from their hundreds and hundreds of ocean-bottom explorations. It was frustrating, discouraging and nearly impossible to get accurate information. But, again and again, day after day, Mel would be on the phone to his investors or encouraging his crew that "Today's the day."

Then, one morning, after all those years of searching and learning and heartbreak, after all those years of begging for funds and pleading with people to believe in his "outrageous" dream, the words came back from the boat: TODAY'S THE DAY!! TODAY IS THE DAY! WE FOUND IT! WE FOUND IT!! IT'S ALL THERE!!!

This incredible story of persistence is one that can inspire us all. Those three words are what you, an independent business owner and/or sales person, believe. Those three words are what keep you going. Today's the day!. Today's the day I get the order!

Comments:

Some customers do not want to drag on and agonize over business decisions. They want to make their decision and then move on to the next problem/crisis. Others are tentative and do not have the confidence to initiate a close to a deal so you have to make it happen. I always worry about the tentative ones so as soon as I get the order signed I leave. If you sit around talking, buyer's remorse can mess up the deal

Crocker Smith

There is tactful, and then there is distasteful. Which we will choose to be? We can be mildly persistant, but we usually know when it is not our day.

Kimberly Burgess

There are some people that cannot be closed no matter what, so while going in with the attitude that it is your day to get the order, we also have to go after that order/close in a non-aggressive manner. Usually, a friendly way to see where I stand is a simple question like "is there anything preventing you from doing business today?" Put the ball in their court to give you their objections – which we then knock off one by one and then again try to get the order.

I always want to leave the customer with the feeling that I am offering them a service that they need, not trying to sell them the last lemon on the lot.

Danielle Antonacci

It seems like a movie. The screen writer has introduced you to the characters , developed the story line , taken you on a roller coaster ride of emotion and intrigue and if he or she fails to bring it all together at the end of the movie you walk away with a let down and a negative opinion of that movie.

The audience expects a proper conclusion …………even demands it.

Alex McQueen

A great example of the difference between "persistence" and "pressure"

I just got a call from Sam's Club. I am a Chamber member and have been asked and asked and asked if I would buy a company or personal Sam's Club Card. My answer was always the same, I am a single mom of three goldens, and my staffing coordinator has a card if we need it for office use.

WELL – the salesperson on the other phone must have thought TODAY WAS HER DAY because I told her my usual response, then told her that a person from the Chamber had marketed to me many times, basically told her I was divorced and barely making enough to live on (of course I worded it differently) then, she STILL told me about the wonderful traveling advantages of the card at hotels and traveling,, etc… finally she even had the nerve to ask me how much I pay for tire rotations because I could get a better deal at Sam's.

After the phone call I felt like I had to defend every answer and come up with an excuse that she approved of, and she even "made" me explain what kind of dog food my three dogs eat. When I got off the phone I felt exhausted and like I had been given the third degree.

I learned that WHEN IT"S NOT YOUR DAY – let it go and try another day.

Angela Brewer

3. When is the best time to close?

Successful closing rests on the solid foundation of planned selling.

Closing the sale should be the easiest step in the sales process when your selling up to this point has been adequate. It is like running the last ten yards for a touchdown after breaking clear of the field. But if by the time you reach the goal line, you have not taken out your interference, it's tough.

It takes confidence and courage to ask for the order and close.

The compelling attitude of unshakable CONFIDENCE on your part when closing is the result of a feeling in your heart that what you have will benefit the customer. As your conscience guides you in conduct, so does this CONFIDENCE intuitively steer your course at the close, directly to the order. If from the time you made your original approach you were careful at each step to ask the buyer questions which indicated your progress, questions which built up favorable admissions, which committed the buyer to positive stands for your proposition, it is then harder for that buyer to begin backing up when you start closing than it is for him to go forward - and easier for you to keep him moving than for him to start back. Again you have the advantage.

The next time you have an opportunity to watch a new sales representative under fire, observe that his or her inexperience is most evident in detecting the right time to start closing.

The time to close can be anytime during the sales call. There is no best time to close. To discover it is to take the sale at the tide and ride in easily. Many times it appears more than once. Sometimes it comes at the outset. The buyer is in the market, knows your line, is ready to buy at once. To go through a complete presentation in this case bores him, and you may talk yourself out of a quick order. In most cases the right time to close appears immediately after you have finished your demonstration and have satisfactorily answered all objections, but you better be sure. Use a trial close at this point to confirm your suspicion that he is ready.

Closing the sales is not as difficult as it is made out to be. If you have done your job of thoroughly explaining your proposition and have clearly created the picture of the prospect using your product or service to enhance their future, the close is simply completing the details.

Planned selling is simply knowing how to lead the prospect, step by step, from getting their attention, creating interest by asking questions and giving testimonials, building desire in their mind by giving a good presentation of what you are selling, and finally moving them toward action by getting them to agree and sign the order or simply say "go ahead and send it to me."

Comments:

After reading this lesson and from my own experiences and observations. It seems safe to assume that each situation is different as well as each customer. You could have similar situations and different customers with opposite personalities, or just the opposite. I think that's what makes my job the most enjoyable, approaching every account and never really knowing what your walking into.

Dominick Yarnal

Every client/sales call is different, so I think that recognizing when to close is a key step in being a success. If you are dead-set on going through your entire presentation, when all you had to do was ask "How many would you like to order?", you are wasting your time, and theirs, and you may even lose the sale. Once you feel the person is interested, and you think that they have all of the info they need, just read t heir signals, and if all signs point to go, then you know what to do!

Laura J. Czajka

The best time. That is a difficult question to answer. I have been in Staffing Sales for 6 years. At this point in my career I just get that feeling it is the right time. It is a difficult comprehension to train people on. I think with each Sales Call you will feel the client out and realize when you need to wrap everything up.

Sometimes that client will close for you. When the client calls your office directly you obviously already have the buy in. They are ready to use your services, now you just have to make sure what you are selling is really what they are looking for. Listen and close.

Danah Parmley

There is no precise formula for the best time to close. If it were that simple we'd have a lot more salespeople in the world! Everything is contextual and each customer is different. Take the time to know what type of sales approach works with different prospects. Some need a little backing off, some need some pushing. Use your instincts and your ability to read people and knowledge of your customer to help you decide when to go for the close.

Timing is everything.

Marquesa Ortega

4. When should you stop talking?

The negative imbalance can swing the decision back. He or she is ready to buy when you are convinced that the DESIRE to own your product or use the service, overbalances the natural inhibitions of fear and indecision. Do not go on talking. You may say something that will help the movement backward. Close! When you see the first SPARK, pile on the fuel until it becomes a blaze ... then stop talking ... make the sale.

Learn to recognize closing signals the buyer sends you. How does he or she tip you off that this is the time to close? By asking for your price at the end of the demonstration, the iron is hot. When the objections stop, that's your cue. Repeated handling of the product is a sure sign. Close inspection of details or enthusiastic questions regarding its application to his particular requirements is another tip. When he turns to an associate and asks her opinion, it is time.

Now appears the ultimate test of your profession, knowing HOW to close when you see the sign that the prospect is ready. The sales person who knows his line and how to present it is still a rank amateur unless he has added the easy technical skill of handling the prospect at this crucial moment. Your buyer now tries to face the great decision. Lead him now into making related MINOR decisions as,

"What pack size do you prefer ... how will I ship this... can I stay over another day and teach your   staff how to sell this. . . will this go through a broker?"

Somewhere during the interview he has indicated an enthusiastic interest in some phase of your proposal. You were wise if you did not use it against him immediately as though you were steering your craft to please him, but held this special interest for major ammunition at the close.

Now use it! If you have been interrupted, sum up the points of your whole demonstration here, particularly if he has called in an associate at the close. Do it anyhow if you are selling to a distributor for resale; the summary suggests selling points the distributor wants for their own resale effort. Hammer away with FACTS at the close. Spot light an appeal to a satisfied user, particularly one he knows. Make him handle, or feel, or smell, or taste ... thus stimulating his possessive instinct. Bring up problems he will meet after the goods are received, as a proper way to market, or where the product will be kept in the warehouse. Use the buying alternative: "Which size would you like... of all of the premiums I offer, which would your manager like best?"

How many times in your life have you bought then and there because of a subtle suggestion by the sales person that someone else will take the article tomorrow if you do not buy now? Don't be timid about ASKING FOR THE

ORDER. He or she expects you to; he or she knows you are not a "greeter" but a person hired to sell.

Comments:

The hardest thing to do is ask for the sale and then to repress the fear that they will say no. So you open your mouth and keep stuttering, rambling on about whatever comes to mind. Ask for the sale and don't make a peep until they answer. The human beings natural tendency is to say yes. Most people do not want to disappoint, so they say yes. If you stop the thought process it gives them the out to say no. Keep your trap shut and let them feel uncomfortable, no matter how long the silence lasts. Let them be the first to talk and you will either get the orfer or get permission to see them again.

Dave Ferren

I think everything has been stated very well here already. One thing that I mentioned earlier is to stop talking after you get the signature on the order. Leave the customer as soon as possible without being rude or short with him. Once you leave, he puts the subject behind him and moves on to his next challenge of running his business. If you sit around talking with him afterwards it is possible that buyer's remorse can slip into his mind, he starts asking more questions and the sale could unravel right before your eyes.

Crocker Smith

Many sales people (especially telemarketers) lose the sale by talking too much. Listening carefully, and being sensitive to the "right moment" in the prospect's mind for him to make a decision should let us know he has all the information necessary to sign the contract.

Paulette Clarke

After you ask your customer for the order and offer a price, don't keep talking yourself into any holes. Give them the burden of coming up with an objection. If you did a good job of selling, they really won't have one. Let them start the negotiating so that you have a jumping off point to counter offer and close the deal. It puts you at a disadvantage if you start whittling your price down before the customer even responds to your offer. So wisely let the customer respond to your initial offer before you go on. Don't be scared to let them mull it over for a few moments.

Marquesa Ortega

Sometimes when both parties are done talking the Sales person tends to continue selling when they don't need to. Many sales people need to realize there is a time to sell and a time to listen. I believe listening to the client enables you to close quicker. If you just continue to talk you will never know whether the customer is ready to close or not.

Make sure and never over talk the customer!!

Danah Parmley

Sometimes I just read a lesson and like it, but can't really come up with something witty to say. I liked this one, and will definitely keep it in mind when I am nervously jabbering about something while I wait for the client to decide what they are doing.

Laura J. Czajka

5. Do you volunteer to cut your price without being asked?

In the real world it is necessary to make price concessions, however, we should be aware of doing it and not lower our price out of habit or fear.

The reason sales people hesitate to ask for what they want is fear of rejection.

Don't fear rejection.

Don't worry about making the customer angry.

Don't be immobilized by your own timidity.

Don't have negative thoughts that will set you up for failure.

"They'll never give up their current supplier and buy from me, so there's no point in even asking."

If you don't make the request the customer is already ahead!

You've made things easy for them! They made the pitch and you bought it!

You've eliminated the possibility that they might say yes or agree to a compromise solution that is equally desirable.

If you are dealing with a person who is not afraid to ask for what they want and you have only a vague idea of what you want, it is like going into a gun fight with no bullets in your gun.

Set your sights high. When you ask for a higher price you allow yourself room to move--trading for other items in the sale you might want during the presentation.

The essence of selling is to make your request loud and clear so the customer hears it.

Don't be afraid to do just that.

Don't be embarrassed to ask for the business.

The compelling attitude of unshakable confidence and positive expectations on your part is the result of a feeling in your heart that what you have will benefit the customer.

As our conscience guides us in conduct, so does CONFIDENCE intuitively steer our course at the close, directly to asking for the price. If from the time you made your original approach you were careful at each step to ask the buyer questions which indicated your progress, questions which built up favorable admissions, which committed the buyer to positive stands for your proposition, it is then harder for that buyer to begin backing up when you start closing than it is for him to go forward. . .and easier for you to keep him moving than for him to start back.

The next time you have an opportunity to watch a new sales representative under fire, observe that his or her inexperience is most evident in asking for the price they would like to get.

Comments:

The first thing to do is have absolute confidence in your product and service. If you don't you can't stand behind the price you charge. Then you immediately fall into the trap of discounting the product. Believe in what you sell and sell the difference to your prospect. If their pricing is close show them the difference in quality. If it is way off the market then either there is a program or they are getting junk. Either way do your homework, junk product is easy to overcome with increased sales and yield. If you can get a cutting then that fixes increased customers. If its junk then do a yield comparison. Don't forget the extra labor to process product . Bingo—you win. If they are too thick in the head after all of this then move on. They won't be there in six months and if they are then the checks will be late—not worth the time.

Dave Ferren

Well I guess I am still a little scared about pricing. I have lowered my price after seeing my cost fall through the floor and was afraid the competitors did too and would come in and bust me. Well that was early on, but here lately I have been sticking to what I have set for them and my profit and sales have been going up.

Jason Kirouac

I sometimes cut my price without being asked. The reason is that I don't want the competitor to come in with a lower price and make me look like I'm over charging them. I only do it on high volume items and on items that I know the customer is keeping a close eye on. Like meats, French fries, cooking oil etc. If you do lower your price on an item you can always make it up on other items like chemicals, coffee and paper products. Every time you lower your price it takes money out of your pocket and the companies. We aren't in the give away business.

Scott Forgie

I try to know the market I am in and the price that it will bear. I hardly cut a price I have quoted immediately. I don't want the customer to know it is that easy or put the thought in their mind that I didn't give them the best price the first time. I will "make the phone call to management" to discuss if we can lower the price this time to get the business.

Danny Swafford

Quoting "list price" first is an effective method. If the price point meets the customers' requirements for size and portion, fits on the menu, why wouldn't they buy it if you properly presented it in every other fashion?

An experienced buyer will try to extract a better price from you, it's their job. Fudging upwards a bit on the list price gives you room to comfortably negotiate with someone who you KNOW is going to take you to the mat trying to nail down a sweet deal. You then have the opportunity to make a profitable sale AND give them what they want.

Chris Chase

Don't offer to cut your price unless the customer absolutely refuses to buy at the price you originally quoted. Don't just assume the customer is going to need a lower price; your original price may be a bargain to them.

David Anderson

The only time I would approach a customer with a lower than normal price would be if we were having a "special" on the product with a discounted price. Many times this will get a customer interested even if he had no thoughts of buying at that time.

But when a customer says "your price is too high", this is a buying signal. It is the perfect time to start closing by saying "where do I need to be to get your business?. If I give you this price will you agree to buy today?". This can greatly accelerate the sale process. The customer has to act one way or the other and you have a much clearer picture of where you stand. It also can close out the competition's involvement in the sale.

Crocker Smith

No way! You should never cut your price until your customer has definitively objected to your rate. If you were interviewing for a job that you knew for a fact had a base salary of 50k, you wouldn't ask for 40k would you? No! When you do get to a point where you are negotiating a lower price, do it in baby steps, small increments. The customer will feel proud they got you to go lower on your price and you will feel better about not sacrificing profits by steeply lowering your rates during the first go round of negotiations.

Marquesa Ortega

No, I don't volunteer to cut my price. The majority of the time I don't volunteer to do this. If a customer asks me to lower the price, or if I can do better, my response is that this is the best I can do. If they try telling me that a competitor has it for $10 cheaper, then asking more questions about the quality, manufacturer, etc of that "comparable" product is what needs to be done. Rolling back on price quickly is not the answer to this common situation. One thing I have learned regarding the price of a product is this - each person that "touches" that product, has to be paid. In my field, that would be at least 10 different people "touching" that product - either directly or indirectly.

JoAnn Welsh

6. The sales process for a new customer presentation?

Do you know the difference between the two distinct types of selling?

The single call close is when you have one opportunity to make the sale. For example, home remodeling. In one 3 or 4 hour period you build rapport, present your product, overcome all the objections, close and leave with the check.

The multiple call close is when you may have to call on a potential account for weeks, or even months, before you are able to build rapport and present your products.

They are two very different types of selling. If you apply the principles of the single call close in a multiply call situation, you will be perceived as "pushy." If you apply the principles of the multiply call close in a single call situation you will starve to death.

If you follow this process to the letter - you will open more new business than you can handle.

You will make more money for you and your family - you will be recognized at the sales meetings - you will win the contest - and you will get your sales manager off your case.

New business is the life of your business. There is no faster way to exceed your sales plan than to aggressively go after new accounts.

If you are having difficulty getting new business it will ALWAYS BE DUE TO ONE OR MORE OF FIVE REASONS.

Learn what they are - work with them - and you will reach your goal.

The sale MUST be made in five steps.

Jump ahead - skip a step - and you will not make the sale.

As I said, if you apply the PRINCIPLES of the single call close to a multiply call close situation you will be perceived as too aggressive and visa versa.

However, the PROCESS is the same.

Here is the PROCESS - THE FIVE STEPS YOU MUST TAKE.

1. YOU MUST SELL YOURSELF FIRST.

As a buyer - if I don't like YOU - I don't care how low your price is - I don't care how well known your company is - I don't care what products you sell. If I don't like you I will not buy from you.

How do you sell yourself?

You have to express more interest in the buyer than anyone ever has. You have to be more interested in them than their own mother. You have to research their business. Find out what their goals and objectives are. Find out what they do in their spare time. Learn the name of their kids and their dog. Find out what their hobbies are. Find out how long they have been in business - how did they get started - what challenges did they have to overcome to reach the level of success they now have.

Until the potential customer feels comfortable with you, don't make the mistake of jumping ahead to the next step. Any attempt to sell a person who is not sold on you first will end in failure and frustration.

This first step may be accomplished in 15 minutes or 15 weeks.

Lets take a lesson from our friends in the car business. If a customer enters the show room and the sales person has not built rapport WITHIN FIFTEEN MINUTES the sales person will pass the customer over to someone else. They know a car will never be sold unless they make it past the first step.

Here are two perfect example of something that happened to me this year - one at a restaurant - one at a store.

My wife and I stopped to have breakfast a few days before Thanksgiving at a Cracker Barrel restaurant. The waitress asked us if we were having company over for Thanksgiving dinner. We said we were having a only few people over. She then suggested that we bring them to the Cracker Barrel for Thanksgiving and save all the work.

She did a perfect job of selling herself first by being interested in whether we were having company rather than simply trying to jump into her pitch about their holiday dinner. It only took her about 15 seconds.

Here is the second example.

I really enjoy a fireplace - but I hate to clean it up and take care of the wood. I stopped at a gas company to ask about a gas burning log they were advertising. As the sales person approached he asked if I had been to Alaska. I didn't realize I was wearing a shirt I had bought while working doing a sales seminar in Alaska. I said yes and for fifteen minutes he asked me questions about my trip.

I was thinking to myself that I really like this guy - he is actually interested in my trip. He sold himself long before we ever started to discuss the benefits of a gas fireplace.

Remember, no one will pay you a penny to listen to your sales pitch. However, consultants are paid thousands of dollars to ask questions.

Don't go into a potential new account and try to sell your company or products until you sell yourself.

2. SELL YOUR COMPANY.

Don't bypass this second step by assuming the prospect knows all about your company. For the prospect to even consider buying from you he or she has to weigh your company against your competitor. They have to make a comparison. They have to know the things that make you different. They need solid facts, not fiction.

Instead of asking, "Are you familiar with our company?" ask, "Do you know much about our company?" Even if your prospects are familiar with your company, they usually don't know much about it. Now you have the opportunity to tell them.

You must be like a lawyer presenting your case to the jury. Don't build your presentation on weak points.

Here you can take a lesson from the folks who sell software. Look on any software box and you will see a "grid." You will see a list of features along the left column. On the top you will see the names of their competitors. By going over this comparison list the potential customer will be presented FACTS AND PROOF that will help them make the decision you want hear.

Never use statements like "we are the biggest" or "we are the best." As soon as you blurt out one of these over used phrases you have immediately unsold yourself. They are thinking, "says who?"

Make a list of at least 20 things you and your company will do for this person once a mutually beneficial program is put together.

3. SELL YOUR PRODUCTS.

Never fall into the trap of giving a price on something when you are in step one or two. Your prospect will probably ask for a price on a specific item. Don't give it to them. Tell them you don't know the price. Tell them you must first learn about their business. You must look at the overall picture. Present your products as solutions to their problems. Always have examples and success stories of other customers who are successfully using your product line.

4. PRESENT YOUR PRICING.

After you have asked a dozen questions and the time has come to suggest products, don't fall into the price trap. If you are more expensive be prepared to JUSTIFY RATHER THAN IMMEDIATELY DISCOUNT.

If your prices are slightly higher than your competitor FIND OUT WHY. What are they leaving out or putting in that is changing the value.

This is the point where you need to know how to negotiate. All buyers want to feel good about making a purchase or changing vendors. You must know how to make them feel good about their decision to change.

5. THE TIMING IS NOT RIGHT.

If you have done a good job of going through the first four steps and the prospect says the timing is not right - then the timing is not right. Find out what their time frame is. Ask for a specific date and time for you to call them back. Don't leave without a follow up plan. If you have NOT done a good job of going through the first four steps THE TIMING WILL NEVER BE RIGHT.

Comments:

I think # 1 is probably the most important of the steps. I guess that stands to reason, if you can't accomplish that one the other points are moot. IF you can accomplish it the others will follow, all the way down to # 5. Sometimes you get a "no" that isn't really a "no", its more like a "wait a minute". It can be frustrating but it is a good idea not to push too hard here.

I have know particular reps at the company I have worked for who spent YEARS getting into an account. They had plenty of time to work on # 1 thru # 4 and all it cost them was a little time. They also established a sense of familiarity and trust that led to those particular accounts being very profitable once they came on board.

Chris Chase

I definitely need to be reminded about the sales process from time to time. It seems like I sometimes skip around and miss steps just to get to the point. I just get excited about the possibility of a new account that I miss things, but I guess this is all a part of being in a sales profession.

Jason Kirouac

I don't believe I ever looked at it as two types of sales calls, single call and the 'farming–planting those seeds' calls. And thank you for taking all those parts of a sales call and placing them in five basic parts of a call. WOW! Those five steps in their right order is what you have to do to make the sales happen.

David Vize

I think, by far, that selling yourself is the most important step. If you are liked you are given more opportunities, more leeway on details of the sale and tolerance for mistakes. I once worked a customer very hard but got nowhere until I realized we had a mutual friend. The door opened and the customer's whole demeanor changed. We had more to talk about and the customer had received a good reference on me. The same thing happened with another customer when I discovered we had the same hobby. Quite a change. These are immediate changes but people can slowly grow to like and trust you over the years after doing business with you. This is the kind of relationship that all salespeople should strive for.

Crocker Smith

When listing the 5 steps, it seems so rigid, but when you read each of the steps in the process of your presentation, it really makes sense, and with a little planning, your prospect won't even realize that you are following them. Instead, they will come out of the call feeling like they just had a really productive conversation with a person/company that is truly interested in helping their business.

Laura J. Czajka

If you cannot sell yourself you it would be very difficult to be a successful sales person. The customer has to buy into you before they buy into what you are offering. If they don't like you, then you are out the door before you can even present anything.

Next step is Sell Your Company. Very important. Need to have the client understanding how great and wonderful your company is before you even present anything else.

Sell Product: Time to let them know why you are there and what you are able to offer. Also at this point very important to listen to the companies needs are. ****In all steps you have to listen to what their needs are.

Pricing: Need to be competitive, but by this time you usually have them understanding you are better than everybody else and whatever rate you are quoting you have to make them realize that Ambassador is worth it. Believe in your product.

Not Right time: Ask when the right time is. Hopefully by this point in the process you will understand their needs and make another appointment to come back when they are ready. Follow up!!

Danah Parmley

This is one of those lessons that I might need to review from time to time. To remind me, all potential accounts you walk into are different but the 5 basic steps remain the same. I think the most important one to remember was " if the timing isn't right then the timing isn't right". Wow have I seen that one mishandled.

Dominick Yarnal

7. Why is it important for you to sell with focus?

Don't say: "This will increase sales."

Instead say: "If you sell 100 of these per week your profit will be over $12,000 per year".

Don't say: "This will lower your labor cost."

Instead say: "This will save you four hours per day in labor cost which will amount to over $7,000 per year in total savings."

Don't use the shotgun approach. Don't try to describe everything you can do in one breath. You've got 3 seconds to get their attention, 30 seconds to tell them why it will benefit them.

Your focus should not be only on products or services. Your focus should be on results such as additional profits, bigger invoice or order sizes, additional customers, lower operating expenses, lower product cost, etc.

In some cases you might want to focus on the results first and the product second. The travel business is a good example. They always focus the results of travel, like the walk on the beach in mid January, or sitting on a lounge chair overlooking the tropical island. They don't tell you about the cramped six-hour plane ride and the 3 hours you have to spend standing in the airport security line.

Your prospect is indifferent. They are thinking about themselves, their problems, their goals, and are completely uninterested in you or your interruption in their day.

Your prospects are exposed to as many as three thousand advertising messages every day. In addition to being interrupted every eight minutes with some type of problem, phone call or employee, they are being called on by hundreds of sales people.

The first three seconds...

You have to say something or show the customer something that will peak their interest in such a way that will make them forget all the things that are currently occupying their mind. What can you do or say that will accomplish this important step in the sale; getting attention? Here are a few examples:

~ Product cost

~ Labor cost

~ Increasing customer base

~ Increasing order size

~ New ideas to help build business

~ Marketing and merchandising ideas

~ New products or services

~ Success stories

~ Their profit and loss statement

~ Solutions to their potential or current problems

~ All are good for getting attention.

What can you say that will swing the prospect's attitude so they will listen with interest what you have to say? You MUST have an opening line that breaks through that attitude and provokes the prospect to say...

"Wow, I'll listen to your story. This is relevant to me and my problems and the goals I am trying to reach! You really know ME and understand MY problems!"

Try focusing on something new. It doesn't necessarily have to be a new product, only new to them. In marketing the word "new" is used over and over again to attract attention. They are always telling about a "new ingredient" or how the product is "new and improved" or it is now in a "new size". Bringing something new to your customers week after week will show them that you are interested in their business by keeping them informed of all the things that are available.

The same is true when talking about percentages. The more you can tie it to a dollar amount the more receptive the customer will be. Don't say "This could lower your cost by one percent". Instead say "this could lower your cost by at least $10,000 per year, which is a full percentage point".

When buying products, customers don't generalize, they think in specifics. The next time you introduce a new product to your accounts, focus on the specifics.

Comments:

I clearly remember selling a customer a specific which changed how I sell. It was dinner rolls and mine were a little less by the case but a much higher quality product. The customer didn't care about the quality he cared about the price. I broke it down by the roll and told him based on the volume of business he would save 25,000 dollars by the time he retired. It was a lot of rolls. Two cents a roll does not seem like a lot of money. On the other hand 25,000 is enough to grab your attention.

Dave Ferren

You start off with "we are the best" and then start the long process of explaining why with facts and specifics. Every company is convinced that they are "the best" and every new prospect does not think that. Along the way, perhaps you convince the prospect that you might be the best in one certain area to the point where they give you an opportunity to prove it by giving you some business. If you are successful and do what you professed to do you should eventually be able to gain most of their business because they will begin to think you really are "the best".

Crocker Smith

This report is all about knowing your stuff basically. You can't just make a general statement, you need to show the client in numbers and in a visual presentation exactly what we can do for them. By having something to show them, we appear to know our business and are willing to go thru the trouble of proving what we say. Know your client, do your research and be prepared.

Kimberly Burgess

Serious customers/prospects will feel you are wasting their time if you cannot focus on specifics. The importance of targeting the right market, and finding something new to share with the prospect each week, is a challenge. But if the fast food and soft drink industries can do it, so can we!

Paulette Clarke

When I am selling I tend to focus on the immediate close. I need to improve and really think about the big picture for the client. Using numbers really seems to work. "You will save $10,000 on your recruiting cost for the first 6 months next year". The sales person's focus needs to be whatever the client's wants and needs are, and every single client is different. I agree with this article. If you aren't able to focus on one goal most sales people will tend oversell the client.

Danah Parmley

Selling with focus, giving the customer the numbers, sounds more like the sales person is the professional, and they know what they are talking about. But you have to be sure that you are giving the customer relative information to their business. Don't just pick a number out of thin air, actually take the time before the meeting to let them know how much dollars this will save them. At the end of the day, the customer doesn't work in percentages, they work in the dollar figure. Giving a comment such as "this will decrease your labour costs" doesn't hold much weight with customers. I found this out first hand!

JoAnne Welch

This lesson takes me back to the lesson about knowing your client or potential client. Some clients are in desperate need of a payroll. Some are fine with their payroll and need quality people to work for them to reduce turn over and costly training. You have to treat each customer individually. I totally agree with your statements about being specific. I took a spreadsheet to a current client and asked for all their business instead of just a small fraction of it. I showed them where they could save more than $20,000 per year by just allowing our company to handle their account exclusively. I use to teach financial statement analysis. Most of the time my students would tell me that sales dropped or expenses rose. I already knew that by looking at the Income statement. I wanted to know WHY!!

Jeffery Mole

About the author Bob Oros

Regardless of whether you are reading one of his books or attending one of his programs, the most frequent comment is: "This guy has been there, he is one of us, I am going to use these strategies."

With over 2,000 speaking engagements in all 50 states and several international locations for manufacturers, distributors and associations, you can be sure you will get the results and information you are looking for. Prior to starting his speaking career, Bob served six years in the US Navy as a Communications Specialist and then worked his way from a street sales person to the position of National Sales Manager for a Fortune 200 company.

Bob has received awards for speaking, writing and marketing too numerous to mention.

Additional Topics by Bob Oros

Why Sales People Fail

The Key to Selling Anybody

The Power of Expectations

Add Value to Every Product

How to Justify Your Price

Lost in 60 Seconds

One Good Reason to Buy

Control a Buyer's Attitude

How to Create Demand

Smoke Screen Objections

Take the Risk Out of Sales

How Small Companies Get Big

www.ingramcontent.com/pod-product-compliance
Lightning Source LLC
Chambersburg PA
CBHW021911170526
45157CB00005B/2043